# Music for the Millennium The Thirties

Music compiled by Peter Evans and Peter Lavender
Song background notes by Michael Kennedy

All text photographs courtesy of Hulton Getty

Cover photograph of Greta Garbo
from The Kobal Collection

Edited by Pearce Marchbank

Text researched and compiled by Heather Page
Book design by Pearce Marchbank and Ben May
Picture research by Nicki Russell

Printed in the United Kingdom by
Page Bros Ltd, Norwich, Norfolk

Exclusive Distributors:
**Music Sales Limited**
8-9 Frith Street,
London W1V 5TZ, England.
**Music Sales Pty Limited**
120 Rothschild Avenue,
Rosebery, NSW 2018,
Australia.

Order No. AM92356
ISBN 0-7119-4432-6
This book © Copyright 1997
by Wise Publications

**Your Guarantee of Quality**
As publishers, we strive to produce every book
to the highest commercial standards.
This book has been carefully designed to minimise
awkward page turns and to make playing from
it a real pleasure.
Particular care has been given to specifying acid-free,
neutral-sized paper made from pulps which have not
been elemental chlorine bleached. This pulp is from
farmed sustainable forests and was produced with
special regard for the environment.
Throughout, the printing and binding have been
planned to ensure a sturdy, attractive publication
which should give years of enjoyment.
If your copy fails to meet our high standards,
please inform us and we will gladly replace it.

Music Sales' complete catalogue describes thousands
of titles and is available in full colour sections by
subject, direct from Music Sales Limited.
Please state your areas of interest and send a
cheque/postal order for £1.50 for postage to:
Music Sales Limited, Newmarket Road, Bury St.
Edmunds, Suffolk IP33 3YB.

Visit the Internet Music Shop at
http://www.musicsales.co.uk

**Wise Publications**
London/New York/Paris/Sydney/Copenhagen/Madrid

Roll up your carpet and
dance at home to the finest
dance band in London.
BBC BROADCAST FROM
THE SAVOY HOTEL FEATURING
THE SAVOY ORPHEANS

How potent
cheap music is.
FROM 'PRIVATE LIVES'
BY NOEL COWARD

There is something
depressing about the way
in which a tram lumbers
and grinds along like a
sick elephant.
J B PRIESTLEY

Write to us about your
woes, whatever they are.
'WOMAN' MAGAZINE'S
ADVICE COLUMN

It's Quicker by Rail.
ADVERTISEMENT FOR LNER

Stop Me and Buy One.
SLOGAN ON WALLS' ICE-CREAM BICYCLES

Filling stations and factories that look like exhibition buildings… giant cinemas and dance-halls and cafés, bungalows with tiny garages, cocktail bars, Woolworths, motor coaches, wireless, hiking, factory girls looking like actresses, greyhound racing and dirt tracks, swimming pools and everything given away for cigarette coupons.
J B PRIESTLEY ON THE NEW ENGLAND IN HIS BOOK 'ENGLISH JOURNEY'

There will be no war this year… or next.
'DAILY EXPRESS', 1939

England is a land of snobbery and privilege, ruled largely by the old and the silly.
GEORGE ORWELL, 1931

I have taken a fairly methodical look in the haberdashers' to see what seems newest and latest in men's wear. Naturally I have only looked in the windows - it would take a Jeanne d'Arc to go further than that. And even the window-gazing had to be fairly swift, since you are apt to be asked to move on if a policeman sees you loitering in Jermyn Street.
ALISON HAIG, FASHION REPORTER IN 'NIGHT AND DAY' MAGAZINE

Truly, the Conservative Party is a wonderful embodiment of good sense, patriotism and honesty.
NEVILLE CHAMBERLAIN, 1931

A remarkable example of engineering and planning, this building is almost devoid of architectural merit. In no place does it rise above the level of a boiler-house.
HUGH CASSON ON THE NEW EARL'S COURT EXHIBITION CENTRE, 1937

If anyone still feels like buying a new car after getting to Earl's Court by road they must have wanted one very badly indeed. Once you're inside, of course, it's very pleasant. Earl's Court is immense and glorious, rather like East Anglia with a roof on - but far more peaceful.
REVIEW IN 'NIGHT AND DAY', 1937

ELIZABETH

MARGARET ROSE

Through one of the marvels of modern science, I am enabled this Christmas Day to speak to all my people throughout the Empire…

GEORGE V BROADCASTING ON THE NEW BBC EMPIRE SERVICE, 1932

I am beginning to think they must like me for myself.

GEORGE V ON THE HUGE CROWDS CELEBRATING THE SILVER JUBILEE, 1935

After I am dead, the boy will ruin himself in twelve months.

GEORGE V ON HIS SON AND HEIR EDWARD

I have found it impossible to carry the heavy burden of responsibility and to discharge my duties as King as I would wish to do without the help and support of the woman I love.

EDWARD VIII IN HIS ABDICATION SPEECH

Hark the herald angels sing Mrs Simpson's pinched our King.

1936 CHILDREN'S VERSION OF THE POPULAR CHRISTMAS CAROL

On the morning of May 12, 1937, two pretty, curly-haired little girls in purple robes and golden coronets stood on a balcony alongside their parents and waved at a cheering crowd. Their Daddy was crowned King of England…they were going to live in a real palace.

'TIME' MAGAZINE

No, it's your mind, lady!
MAX MILLER, THE 'CHEEKY CHAPPIE'

It is not a question of censorship. It is a question of decency. Some modern books are quite all right, those about travel and those about Sussex, but others ought not to be available.
LONDON 'EVENING STANDARD', 1937

Counsel's opinion was taken as to the definition of a couple 'lying in bed'. Lawyers finally propounded the theory that a couple were 'in bed' when both pairs of feet were off the ground.
CHARLES GRAVES ON FILM CENSORSHIP IN 'THE SPHERE'

It gave the illusion that the participants were threading their way along the ledges of dangerous precipices...
BEVERLEY NICHOLS ON THE TANGO CRAZE

Our true intent is all for your delight.
SLOGAN FOR BUTLIN'S FIRST HOLIDAY CAMP, SKEGNESS, 1937

Nothing over sixpence.
WOOLWORTH'S SLOGAN

I'm afraid it's unlikely that anyone, least of all the BBC, would notice me taking off my hat; but I raise it in the hope that the existence of one grateful listener may be an encouragement to Victor Silvester and his Band to continue to play without the help of vocalists …
I find it difficult to believe that anyone . .. would miss very much … such a ban would be effective enough if it amounted to no more than forbidding the broadcast of certain rhymes, e.g. Baby: Maybe, Moon: Soon, Remember: December, Blew: Yew …
JOHN HAYWARD IN
'NIGHT AND DAY' MAGAZINE

Of Toscanini there is as usual little to say. Either you think him the greatest conductor alive or else you don't, in which latter case you're wrong.
CONSTANT LAMBERT IN
'NIGHT AND DAY' MAGAZINE

It will chill you and fill you with fears. You'll find it creepy and cruel and crazed.
'THE NEW YORK TIMES' ON THE FILM 'DRACULA', 1931

I am speaking to you from the Cabinet Room at 10, Downing Street. This morning the British Ambassador in Berlin handed the German government a final note stating that unless we heard from them by eleven o'clock that they were prepared to withdraw their troops from Poland a state of war would exist between us. I have to tell you now that no such undertaking has been received and consequently this country is at war with Germany.
NEVILLE CHAMBERLAIN SEPTEMBER 1939

The Home Office announces that the designing of gas masks has been difficult but this has been surmounted and production is now in hand.
GOVERNMENT ANNOUNCEMENT, 1938

Players Please.
CIGARETTE ADVERTISEMENT, 1937

*It took four people to compose the 1930 hit 'Bye Bye Blues'. One of them was the now rarely remembered band leader Bert Lowe, who adopted it as his signature tune. Thirty-five years later, popular German bandleader Bert Kaempfert enjoyed his one and only British Top Thirty hit with the song.*

# Bye Bye Blues

Words & Music by Bert Lowe, Chauncey Gray, David Bennett & Fred Hamm.

There's on-ly hap-pi-ness for me. So,

Bye Bye Blues, _____ Bye

Bye Blues. _____ Bells ring,

birds sing, Sun is shin - ing, no more

# Falling In Love Again

Music & Original Words by Friedrich Hollander.
English Words by Reg Connelly.

The Blue Angel was the 1930 German film that brought international fame to Marlene Dietrich. Its decadent setting in the sleazy night-clubs of pre-war Germany was revolutionary in its time. The songs, by Friedrich Hollander, captured the world-weary cynicism of the time. And one - 'Falling in Love Again', with English words by Reg Connelly - became a standard.

*CHORUS*

*One of the happiest of all popular songs, 'On The Sunny Side Of The Street' is further testimony to the songwriting talent of Jimmy McHugh and Dorothy Fields. It surfaced in The International Revue on Broadway, and was soon snapped up for the movies - including Ted Lewis's Is Everybody Happy? as well as both The Benny Goodman Story and The Eddie Duchin Story.*

# On The Sunny Side Of The Street

Words by Dorothy Fields. Music by Jimmy McHugh.

# Where The Blue Of The Night Meets The Gold Of The Day

Words & Music by Roy Turk, Fred Ahlert & Bing Crosby.

Bing Crosby was one of many stars of The Big Broadcast, a 1932 film musical revue. The plot concerned a failing radio station that was saved by the intervention of a series of stars. Bing co-wrote his own song 'Where The Blue Of The Night Meets The Gold Of The Day' and it became his signature tune. The other writers were lyricist Roy Turk and composer/arranger Fred E. Ahlert.

23

only I could see her,⎯⎯⎯⎯⎯ oh, how hap - py I would be!⎯⎯⎯⎯⎯⎯⎯⎯⎯ Where the blue of the night meets the gold of the day, some - one waits for

**1.** me.⎯⎯⎯⎯⎯ Where the **2.** me.

# Wrap Your Troubles In Dreams
## (And Dream Your Troubles Away)

Words by Ted Koehler & Billy Moll. Music by Harry Barris.

*Harry Barris, a former member of Paul Whiteman's vocal group The Rhythm Boys in the Twenties, appeared in many films, and led his own dance band. In 1931, with Ted Koehler and Billy Moll he created the song 'Wrap Your Troubles In Dreams'. It was featured in the films Top Man (1943) and Rainbow Round My Shoulder (1957), the latter featuring singing star Frankie Laine.*

In slow rhythmic tempo

VERSE

What price hap-pi-ness? What price hap-pi-ness? Who can truth-ful-ly say? But for ev-'ry share, with tears we pay. Love is hap-pi-ness! I've had hap-pi-ness,

But it end-ed one day, Now I look at life a diff-'rent

way.

CHORUS

When skies are cloud-y and grey, They're

on-ly grey for a day, So wrap your trou-bles in

dreams And dream your trou-bles a - way. Un -

til that sun-shine peeps through    There's on-ly one thing to do,    Just wrap your trou-bles in dreams    And dream your trou-bles a-way.    Your cas-tles may tum-ble, that's fate af-ter all,___    Life's real-ly fun-ny that way,

# Underneath The Arches

### Words & Music by Bud Flanagan.

'Underneath The Arches' was written by one half of the comedy duo (Bud) Flanagan and (Chesney) Allen. Both were seasoned musical performers before their first performance together in Birkenhead where they first performed their signature tune. It was used as the title song of their 1937 film, and was also the name of a successful tribute show just a few years ago.

arch - es,_____ I dream my dreams a - way,_____ un - der-neath the

arch - es,_____ on cob - ble-stones I lay,_____ ev - 'ry night you'll

find me,_____ ti - red out and worn,_____ hap - py when the

day - light comes creep - ing, her - ald - ing the dawn. Sleep - ing when it's

raining, and sleeping when it's fine, I hear the trains rattling

by above, pavement is my pillow, no matter where I

stray, underneath the arches, I dream my dreams a-

**1.**
way.

**2. & Fine**
Underneath the way.

*opt: D.%. al Fine*

# I'm Gettin' Sentimental Over You

Words by Ned Washington. Music by Geo. Bassman.

Ned Washington and George Bassman wrote 'I'm Gettin' Sentimental Over You' in 1932. Washington was a popular lyricist, contributing to stage and screen successes from the Twenties to the Sixties. Composer George Bassman was an arranger for films, and recordings. 'I'm Getting Sentimental Over You' was adopted as his signature tune by bandleader Tommy Dorsey.

I was just an-oth-er who laughed at ro-mance,— I said it was not for me.—
Nev-er was a dream-er un-til I met you,— fun-ny how one gets that way.—

Then you made your en-trance and right at a glance,— I knew this was meant for me.—
Cu-pid's just a schem-er and I nev-er knew,— now I'm dream-ing dreams all day.—

34

# Don't Blame Me

Words & Music by Jimmy McHugh & Dorothy Fields.

1. Ev-er since the luck-y night I found you— I've hung a-round you,— just like a
2. I like ev-'ry sin-gle thing a-bout you— With-out a doubt you— are like a

fool
dream.
Fall-ing head and heels in love like a kid out of
In my mind I find a pic-ture of us as a

school
team.

My poor heart is in an aw-ful state now___ But it's too
Ev-er since the hour of our meet-ing___ I've been re-

late now___ to call a halt.
peat-ing___ a sil-ly phrase

So if I be-come a
Hop-ing that you'll un-der-

nui-sance
stand me

it's all
one of

your fault!
these days.

Don't blame

me

for fall-ing in love with you

I'm un-der your spell but

# Stars Fell On Alabama

Words by Mitchell Parish. Music by Frank Perkins.

*Salem, Massachusetts-born Frank Perkins was responsible for the music for a few choice songs. As a conductor/arranger, he lived in Hollywood, working on June Haver and Doris Day films. In 1934 he collaborated with Louisiana's Mitchell Parish on 'Stars Fell On Alabama'. The many recordings of this song include a classic by Billie Holiday.*

Moon-light and mag-no-lia, star-light in your hair, all the world a dream come true,

did it real-ly hap-pen, was I real-ly there, was I real-ly there with you?

41

na - tion— a si - tu - a - tion— so hea - ven - ly,— a fai - ry land where no one else could

en - ter,— and in the cen - tre— just you and me, dear; my heart beat like a

ham - mer, my arms wound a - round you tight, and stars fell on A - la -

**1.**
ba - ma last night.

**2.**
night.

42

# My Very Good Friend
# The Milkman

Words by Johnny Burke. Music by Harold Spina.

*New York-born Harold Spina collaborated with California born lyricist Johnny Burke, who was of Irish extraction. 'My Very Good Friend The Milkman' was a hit for larger-than-life singer/pianist Thomas 'Fats' Waller who had the honour of making this song his own. Its joyous, sly ebullience was ideally suited to Waller's bubbly personality.*

# East Of The Sun (And West Of The Moon)

### Words & Music by Brooks Bowman

*Brooks Bowman is one of the forgotten men of music, whose reputation rests on two songs, 'Love And A Dime' and 'East Of The Sun (And West Of The Moon)'. The latter was written in 1935, and has enjoyed memorable recordings by Frank Sinatra with Tommy Dorsey, The Inkspots, Peggy Lee, Lee Wiley and Dinah Shore.*

Slowly, With Expression

The film Pennies From Heaven was a 1936 charmer in which Bing Crosby befriended a little girl who had no home. There was a magnificent crop of songs and the title tune by Johnny Burke and Arthur Johnston was nominated for an Academy Award. In 1981 a second film of the same name was the film version of Dennis Potter's highly acclaimed television series.

# Pennies From Heaven

Words by John Burke. Music by Arthur Johnston.

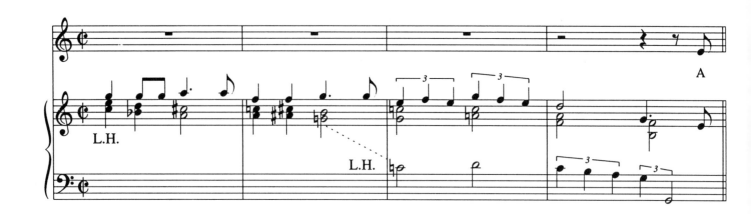

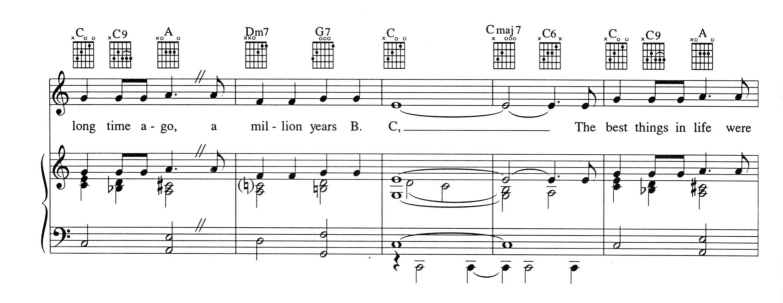

long time a-go, a mil-lion years B. C, ___ The best things in life were

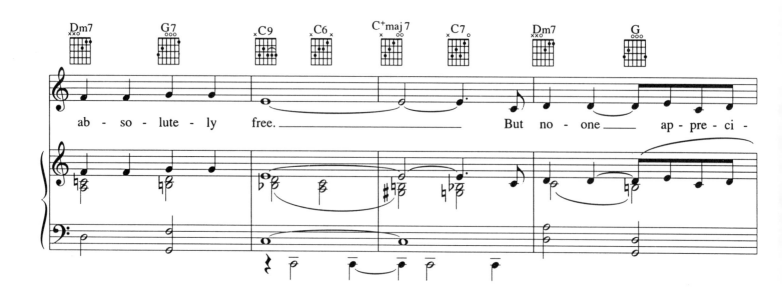

ab-so-lute-ly free. ___ But no-one ___ ap-pre-ci-

*Composer and lyricist Billy Hill wrote many successful songs, many of which had a Western flavour; yet he was born and died in Boston, Massachusetts, on America's eastern seaboard. Hill's songs almost always were nostalgic, summoning up images of a forgotten past. His 1936 hit 'In the Chapel In The Moonlight' is an enduring standard.*

# In The Chapel In The Moonlight

Words & Music by Billy Hill.

# The Touch Of Your Lips

### Words & Music by Ray Noble.

British bandleader Ray Noble was for
many years Artists and Repertoire Manager
for HMV, during which time he ran the finest
studio-based dance band of all.
During this time, and following his
successful move to America,
Noble found time to write some excellent songs.
'The Touch Of Your Lips' immediately became
a standard with many fine recordings,
notably one by Nat 'King' Cole.

Moderately Slow with expression

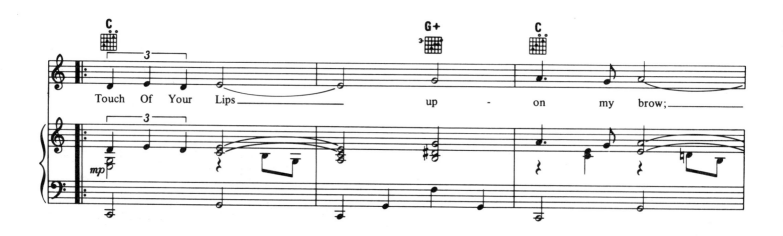

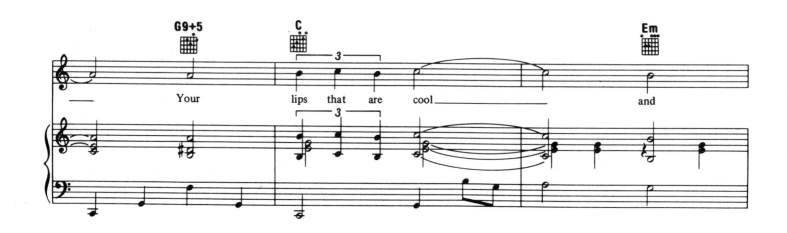

# The Way You Look Tonight

Music by Jerome Kern. Words by Dorothy Fields.

Swing Time, one of the finest of all Fred Astaire-Ginger Rogers pictures, featured Fred as a gambler/dancer, Ginger a dance instructress. At one point, Fred serenaded Ginger (who was off-screen in another room shampooing her hair). Music for the song was written by Jerome Kern and the lyrics were provided by Dorothy Fields. 'The Way You Look Tonight' deservedly won the Oscar for best song of its year.

glow just think - ing of you,
for me but to love you,

and the way you look to - night._____
just the way you look to - night._____

Oh, but you're

With each

# All The Things You Are

Music by Jerome Kern. Words by Oscar Hammerstein II.

Very Warm For May opened on Broadway in November 1939, closing the following January. May was the heroine, chased by gangsters - hence it was very warm for her! The show contained one of the finest songs of that - or of any - year, 'All The Things You Are', which subsequently featured in the 1944 film Broadway Rhythm.

Moderately, with expression

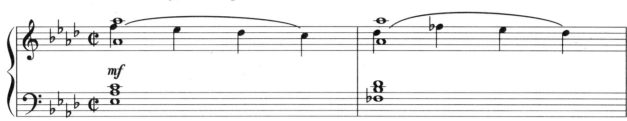

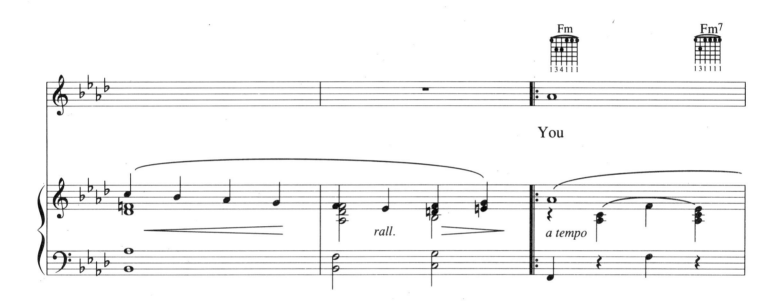

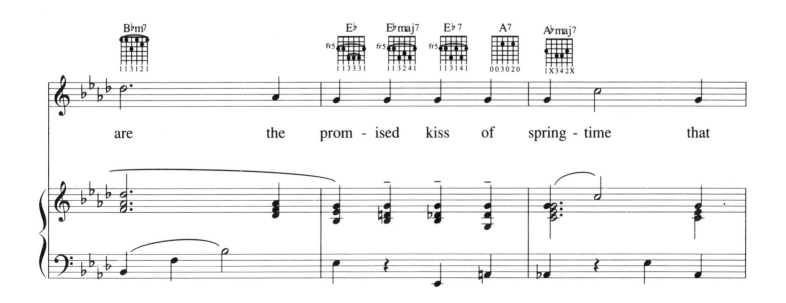

are. _____ Some

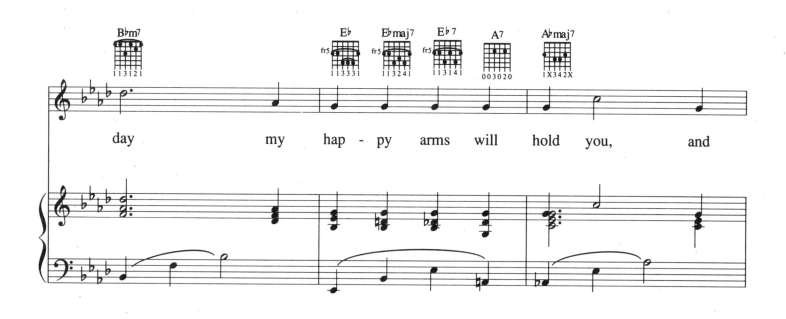

day my hap - py arms will hold you, and

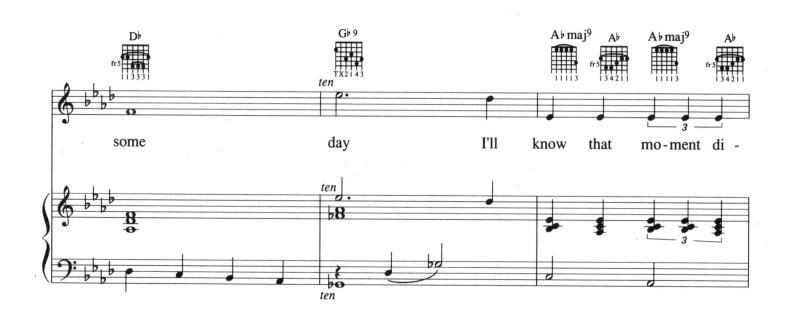

some day I'll know that mo - ment di -

vine, when all the things you are, are

mine!

mine!

# South Of The Border

Words & Music by Jimmy Kennedy & Michael Carr.

'South Of The Border (down Mexico Way)' is a British song from 1939, written by the well-known team of Michael Carr and Jimmy Kennedy who were separately and together responsible for some of the best known novelties and romantic ballads of the 30s and 40s. It was not only a British hit; Bing Crosby also made a memorable hit recording of the song.